Half Wit

summersdale

HALF WIT

Summersdale Publishers Ltd
46 West Street
Chichester
West Sussex
PO19 1RP
UK

www.summersdale.com

Printed and bound in Great Britain

ISBN: 978-1-84024-693-3

Disclaimer
Every effort has been made to attribute the quotations in this collection to the correct source. Should there be any omissions or errors in this respect we apologise and shall be pleased to make the appropriate acknowledgements in any future editions.

Half Wit

Aubrey Malone

Contents

Editor's Note

We all suffer from lapses in concentration when it would appear that our speech and intellect are working independently from one another. This book is dedicated to those such instances and provides the opportunity to laugh at the expense of the poor unfortunates whose public faux pas will forever come back to haunt them.

'Foot in Mouth' appears to be particularly prevalent in the public arena, and virulent strains seem to have ravaged the minds of not only intellectuals but a fair few pseudo-intellectuals and downright dumb individuals too. Perhaps there's something in the water in the corridors of power and the media institutions – or maybe the MPs and press are just a few sandwiches short of a picnic.

From sports commentators who clearly need their eyes checked to TV presenters who should have done their homework, laugh yourself silly at their mindless meanderings and cringeworthy cock-ups. It just goes to confirm that these people are only human after all.

BROKEN ENGLISH

'If' is a very large
preposition.

John Major

I deny the allegations and
I defy the alligators!

Indicted Chicago Alderman

It's a conflict of parallels.

Alex Ferguson

I couldn't fail to disagree
with you less.

Fran O'Shea

That tie is a potential potato skin.

Alan Hansen

———— ◆ ————

I answer in the affirmative
with an emphatic 'No'.

Sir Boyle Roche

———— ◆ ————

You know what they say:
don't get mad, get angry.

Edwina Currie

I can drink like
a chimney.

Alex Ferguson

Mr Milosevic has to be careful.
The calendar is ticking.

Richard Haas

———

A zebra doesn't change its spots.

Al Gore

———

The crowd gave the players
an arousing reception.

Packie Bonner

I have a thermometer in my mouth
and I'm listening to it all the time.

Willie Whitelaw

I'm absolutely thrilled and
over the world about it.

Tessa Sanderson

We'll be heading for the
deepening heights of recession.

Economic spokesman

That's just the tip of the ice cube.

Neil Hamilton

I understand the importance of
bondage between parent and child.

Dan Quayle

I cannot tell you how grateful I
am – I am filled with humidity.

Gib Lewis

Everybody line up alphabetically
according to their height.

Casey Stengel

It's great to be back on terra cotta.

John Prescott

I would like to thank the press
from the heart of my bottom.

Nick Faldo

I think they've
misunderestimated me.

George W. Bush

DID I REALLY
SAY THAT?

Politics gives guys
so much power that
they tend to behave
badly around women.
And I hope I never
get into that.

Bill Clinton

I'm using my brain for the
first time in a long time.

Victoria Beckham

❖

Beyond its entertainment value,
Baywatch has enriched and,
in many cases, saved lives.

David Hasselhoff

❖

You can tell a lot about a
man's character by the way
he eats jelly beans.

Ronald Reagan

Originally my mother was
Spanish. Then she became
a Jehovah's Witness.

Geri Halliwell

I didn't know 'Onward Christian
Soldiers' was a Christian song.

Aggie Pate

I think we should
put contraception
on the long finger.

Jack Lynch

I strongly support the
feeding of children.

Gerry Ford

———— ◆ ————

I used to think oral sex was
just thinking about it.

James McKeown

———— ◆ ————

Illegitimacy is something we should
talk about in terms of not having it.

Dan Quayle

FOOT IN MOUTH

The Miss World
contest is still popular
even if it has its fair
share of knockers.

Julia Morley

I stand for anti-bigotry, anti-racism and anti-Semitism.

George W. Bush

◆

I want all the kids to copulate me.

Andre Dawson

◆

We would have no coal industry if the miners are driven into the ground.

Claire Brooks

We've got to pause and
ask ourselves: how much
clean air do we need?

Lee Iacocca

———

Sometimes they write what I
say and not what I mean.

Pedro Guerrero

———

People say I swear a lot.
That's bollocks.

Charlotte Church

Anyone buying
this record can be
assured that the
money they pay will
literally be going into
someone's mouth.

Bob Geldof

I've got taste.
It's inbred in me.

David Hasselhoff

You know what's wrong with
this country? Everyone gets a
chance to have their fair say.

Bill Clinton

DON'T FOLLOW
THE SIGNS

Beware: to touch
these wires is
instant death.
Anyone found doing
so will be prosecuted.

Sign at Donegal Electric Station

All ice cubes should be
boiled before using.

US Army notice during typhoid epidemic

Today's launch has been
called off due to flooding.

Notice outside a Clyde shipyard

To avoid breakage, keep
bottom on top.

Instruction on carton

Midnight bowling at 9 p.m.

Bowling alley sign

Permitted vehicles not allowed.

Road sign on US 27

Caution: cape does not enable user to fly.

Warning label on a Batman costume

BALLS-UPS

Strangely in slow
motion replay, the ball
seemed to hang in the
air for even longer.

David Acfield

As with every young
player, he's only 18.

Alex Ferguson

Graeme Souness went behind
my back right in front of my face.

Craig Bellamy

Without picking out anyone
in particular, I thought Mark
Wright was tremendous.

Graeme Souness

He's had two cruciates and a
broken ankle. That's not easy.
Every player attached to the club
is praying the boy gets a break.

Alex Ferguson on Wes Brown

❖

I never comment on referees and
I'm not going to break the habit
of a lifetime for that prat.

Ron Atkinson

❖

There will be more football in
a moment, but first we've got
the highlights of the Scottish
League Cup Final.

Gary Newbon

People slag me off about
my right foot, but without it
I couldn't use my left.

John Morley

—◦—

The fans like to see Balde
wear his shirt on his sleeve.

Kenny Dalglish

—◦—

Arsenal are streets ahead of
everyone in the Premiership, and
Man United are up there with them.

Craig Bellamy

I watched the game, and
saw an awful lot of it.

Andy Gray

———•———

Who should be there at the far post
but yours truly, Alan Shearer.

Colin Hendry

———•———

There was a bit of retaliation
there, though not actually
on the same player.

Frank Stapleton

I don't have a normal life, but for me
there's nothing in it that isn't normal.

Ryan Giggs

———·———

England have the best fans in
the world, and Scotland's ones
are also second to none.

Kevin Keegan

———·———

There's a lot of good older
players around, but very few.

David Carr

He dribbles a lot and the opposition don't like it – you can see it all over their faces.

Ron Atkinson

The word 'genius' isn't applicable
in football. A genius is a guy
like Norman Einstein.

Joe Theismann

❦

He sliced the ball when
he had it on a plate.

Ron Atkinson

❦

The tide is very much
in our court now.

Kevin Keegan

I felt a lump in
my mouth as the
ball went in.

Terry Venables

WHERE ON EARTH?

China is a big
country, inhabited
by many Chinese.

Charles de Gaulle

So, Woosie, you're from Wales.
What part of Scotland is that?

American journalist to Ian Woosnam
during a 1987 press conference

Playing with wingers is more effective
against European sides like Brazil
than English sides like Wales.

Ron Greenwood

What state is Wales in?

George W. Bush to Charlotte Church

So where's the Cannes film
festival being held this year?

Christina Aguilera

———◆———

I came to Nantes two years ago
and it's much the same today except
that it's completely different.

Brian Moore

———◆———

Mum, have I sung at the
Hollywood Bowl?

Charlotte Church

Moving from Wales to Italy is like moving to a different country.

Ian Rush

I've read about foreign policy and studied. I now know the number of continents.

George Wallace

Sarajevo isn't Hawaii.

Bobby Robson

Where is East Angular,
is it abroad?

Jade Goody

I've never really wanted to go to
Japan, simply because I don't
like eating fish. And I know that's
very popular out there in Africa.

Britney Spears

DUMBING DOWN

We shouldn't let the
government off the
hook just when we
have it on the run.

Helen Goodman

I want to make sure everybody
who has a job wants a job.

George W. Bush

———

Solutions are not the answer.

Richard Nixon

———

The American public wants a
solemn ass for president, and I
think I'll go along with them.

Calvin Coolidge

If Abraham Lincoln were alive
today, he'd roll over in his grave.

Gerald Ford

The government will never accept
an acceptable level of violence.

Patrick Donegan

Those of us who
spent time in the
agricultural sector
understand how unfair
the death penalty is.

George W. Bush

A week is a long time in politics.
Three weeks is twice as long.

Rosie Barnes

Half the lies our opponents
tell about us are untrue.

Sir Boyle Roche

We've got a strong candidate.
I'm trying to think of his name.

**Connecticut senator Christopher
Dodd on his colleague**

LOST IN TRANSLATION

Do the French
have a word for
'entrepreneur'?

George W. Bush

Pepsi brings your ancestors
back from the grave.

Translation of 'Come Alive with Pepsi' in Hong Kong

No Need for Any Doctors

Translation of *Dr No* in Japan

Four people were killed,
one seriously.

Japan Times

Persons are requested not to
occupy seats without consummation.

Notice in a Spanish cafe

Teeth extracted by the
latest Methodists.

Sign in a Hong Kong dentist's surgery.

Danger Slow Men at Work

Road sign in Brunei

I was recently on a
tour of Latin America,
and the only regret
I have was that I
didn't study Latin
harder in school so
I could converse
with those people.

Dan Quayle

SPORTING GAFFES

If golf wasn't my
living, I wouldn't play
it if you paid me.

Christy O'Connor

The Koreans were quicker
in terms of speed.

Mark Lawrenson

***

Look at Stephen Hendry
sitting there totally focussed,
just staring into space.

David Vine

***

The line-up for the final of the
women's 400-metre hurdles includes
three Russians, two East Germans,
a Pole, a Swede and a Frenchman.

David Coleman

You guys pair up in groups of three, then line up in a circle.

Bill Peterson

The lead car is absolutely unique, except for the one behind which is identical.

Murray Walker

Are there any more
great swimmers in
the pipeline?
Cliff Morgan

I'll fight Lloyd Honeyghan for
nothing if the price is right.

Marlon Starling

❖

Playing another side could be an
omen, but I don't believe in omens.

George Graham

❖

There's nothing wrong with the
car except that it's on fire.

Murray Walker

I was in a no-win situation so I'm
glad I won rather than lost.

Frank Bruno

The Queen's Park Oval, exactly as
the name suggests, absolutely round.

Tony Cozier

SMART ARSE

What a waste it is
to lose one's mind.
Or not to have a mind
is being very wasteful.

Dan Quayle

Facts are stupid things.

Ronald Reagan

—◆—

I thought I was wrong,
but I was mistaken.

Dan O'Herlihy

—◆—

I'm not very clever, but
I'm quite intelligent.

Dirk Bogarde

Trees cause more
pollution than
automobiles do.

Ronald Reagan

PFFFTT

I have opinions of my own,
strong opinions, but I don't
always agree with them.

George W. Bush

Richard Burton has a
tremendous passion for the
English language, especially
the spoken and written word.

Frank Bough

I have a God-given talent.
I got it from my dad.

Julian Wakefield

WAR REPORTS

We cannot let
terrorists and rogue
nations hold this
nation hostile or hold
our allies hostile.

George W. Bush

I'm honoured to shake
the hand of a brave
Iraqi citizen who had
his hand cut off by
Saddam Hussein.

George W. Bush

The Libyan army is capable
of destroying America
and breaking its nose.

Muammar al-Qaddafi

Osama Bin Laden is either
alive and well, or alive and
not too well, or not alive.

Donald Rumsfeld

We are not at war with Egypt.
We are in armed conflict.

Anthony Eden

I think war is a dangerous place.

George W. Bush

DOH!

Not only is he
ambidextrous, but
he can throw with
either hand.

Duffy Daugherty

That's a self-portrait of
himself by himself.

Richard Madeley

❦

And now, excuse me while
I interrupt myself.

Murray Walker

❦

Did you find yourself reminiscing a
great deal in your autobiography?

Gloria Hunniford

Babies are so
human – they remind
one of monkeys.

Saki

So, if you've got a birthday coming
up in the next twelve months or so...

Lynda Berry

I don't know what impressive is,
but Joe was impressive tonight.

Marlene Bugner

The Everly Brothers
died ten years ago.

Don Everly at their farewell concert

Some man sent me condoms
and underpants in the post.
I'm not sure what he wanted.

Martine McCutcheon

❦

We will be an aggressive opposition
where we oppose things, and we'll
support things that we support.

Bertie Ahern

❦

Most cars on the roads have only
one occupant, usually the driver.

Carol Malia

Traditionally, most of Australia's
imports come from overseas.

Keppel Enderbery

I think that gay marriage should
be between a man and a woman.

Arnold Schwarzenegger

There'll be no siestas
in Madrid tonight.

Kevin Keegan

I used to think a
socialist was someone
who went out a lot.

George Best

DUMB AND DUMBER

If I could read a
book, I'd definitely
read one of yours.

Paris Hilton

The illiteracy level of our
children are appalling.

George W. Bush

Always go to other people's
funerals, otherwise they
won't come to yours.

Yogi Berra

My sister's expecting a baby,
and I don't know if I'm going
to be an uncle or an aunt.

Chuck Nevitt

He's a guy who gets up at
six o'clock in the morning
regardless of what time it is.

Lou Duva

—•—

We are trying to change
the 1974 Constitution,
whenever that was passed.

Donald Ray Kennard

—•—

We're definitely going to get
Brooklyn christened, but we
don't know into which religion.

David Beckham

I never mind whether
restaurants serve
white wine or red.
I'm colour blind.

Dudley Moore

MIXED MESSAGES

This play will be repeated tomorrow night, so that those who missed it will have the opportunity of doing so again.

Sign outside a Dublin theatre

Hot and cold baths under
personal supervision
of the proprietor.

Notice in a Blackpool guest-house

All water in this establishment has
been passed by the manager.

Sign in a Dundee cafeteria

An alternative to good eating.

Restaurant business card in Texas

Don't squeeze
the fruit here – ask
for Debbie.

Street stand warning

Free admission for old age
pensioners if accompanied
by both parents.

Sign outside a Scottish cinema

Leave your clothes here and
go out and enjoy yourself.

Offer in an Edinburgh laundrette

Ladies are requested not to
have children at the bar.

Sign in a Norwegian cocktail lounge

Wonderful bargains
for men with 16
and 17 necks.

Sign at a men's clothing store

POP TARTS

I'm a really big Elvis
fan. I think the reason
we did the whole
Elvis thing was
because, you know,
he's from Vegas.

Britney Spears

Culture Club never actually split up.
We just stopped speaking to each
other and went our separate ways.

Boy George

—•—

Oasis aren't arrogant.
We just think we're the
best band in the world.

Noel Gallagher

—•—

I'm not anorexic. I'm from Texas.
Are there people from Texas that
are anorexic? I've never heard of one.

Jessica Simpson

I don't walk. I sort of tumble.
My legs are always trying to
catch up with my head.

Ozzy Osbourne

My second hit was a flop.

Shakin' Stevens

I'm still friends with all my exes,
apart from my husbands.

Cher

I hate music, especially
when it's played.

Jimmy Durante

Twenty-three is old. It's almost 25
which is, like, almost mid-twenties.

Jessica Simpson

THE RAVING
LOONY PARTY

All I was doing
was appealing for
an endorsement,
not suggesting
you endorse it.

George W. Bush

For NASA, space is
still a high priority.

Dan Quayle

———❦———

I believe there would be people alive
today if there were a death penalty.

Nancy Reagan

———❦———

I believe we're on an irreversible
trend towards more freedom and
democracy. But that could change.

Dan Quayle

I know how hard it is to put
food on your family.

George W. Bush

That scoundrel deserves to be
kicked to death by a jackass,
and I'm just the one to do it.

Texan Congressional candidate

The Tory party only
panics in a crisis.

Iain MacLeod

I'm not going to have some reporters pawing through our papers. We are the president.

Hillary Clinton

First, let me make it absolutely clear: poor people aren't necessarily killers.

George W. Bush

OWN GOALS

The last time we played Seville we were beaten two-nil. And we were lucky to get nil.

Mick McCarthy

It will be a shame if either side lose.
And that applies to both sides.

Jock Brown

It's one of the greatest goals
ever, but I'm surprised that
people are talking about it
being the goal of the season.

Andy Gray

Neville Southall was the finest
goalkeeper I ever came up against –
even though I always seemed to have
the knack of scoring against him.

Ian Rush

If Ireland finish with a draw in winning
the game, that would be fine.

Jack Charlton

❦

Ian Rush unleashed his left foot
and it hit the back of the net.

Mike England

❦

Winning doesn't really matter
as long as you win.

Vinnie Jones

We're not going to win
if we don't score.

Dave Lewis

Some of the goals were good,
some of the goals were sceptical.

Bobby Robson

An inch or two either side
of the post and that would
have been a goal.

Dave Bassett

LOUSY PREDICTIONS

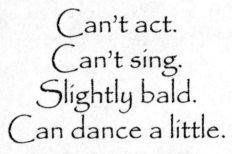

Can't act.
Can't sing.
Slightly bald.
Can dance a little.

Screen test report on Fred Astaire

For the majority of people, the use of tobacco has a beneficial effect.

Ian G. MacDonald in 1969

Gone With the Wind is going to be the biggest flop in Hollywood history. I'm just glad it'll be Clark Gable who's falling flat on his face and not me.

Gary Cooper

A flash in the pan.

Billboard magazine on Madonna in 1983

We don't like their sound.
Anyway, guitar music
is on the way out.

Decca Recording Company on The Beatles

Elvis can't last.

Jackie Gleason in 1956

Silent pictures will last for ever.
Who the hell wants to
hear actors talk?

Harry Warner

I fear that the development
of the railway will destroy the
need for waterproof coats.

Charles MacIntosh

The French people are
incapable of regicide.

King Louis XVI in 1789

Anyone who looks for a source
of power in the transformation of
the atom is talking moonshine.

Lord Rutherford in 1936

No matter what happens,
the US Navy is not going
to be caught napping.

**Frank Knox, the day before the
invasion of Pearl Harbour**

They couldn't hit an
elephant at this dist–

The last words of Union General Sedgwick

There's no way I'll allow Marlon
Brando to play Don Corleone.
He's box office poison.

Casting executive of *The Godfather*

112

Everything that can be
invented has been invented.

Charles H. Duell in 1899

Computers in the future
may have only 1,000 vacuum
tubes and perhaps only weigh
one and a half tons.

Popular Mechanics, 1949

You'd better learn secretarial
work or else get married.

Modelling agency director Emmeline Snively's
advice to Marilyn Monroe in 1944

When the Paris
Exhibition closes,
electric light will close
with it and no more
will be heard of it.

Erasmus Wilson

IT DOESN'T ADD UP

My average weekly
velocity is 50 miles
an hour, including
right now, when
I'm standing still.

Marlon Brando

If crime went down 100 per
cent, it would still be 50 times
higher than it should be.

John Bowman

—◆—

We're overpaying him,
but he's worth it.

Samuel Goldwyn

—◆—

It's a one-to-one dialogue.
You open your mouth and you're
talking to six million people.

Derek Jameson

Of the designs of mine that
succeed, 50 per cent of them don't.

Zandra Rhodes

—•—

Half this game is
90 per cent mental.

Danny Ozark

—•—

Coming onto the pitch is
Mike Moore, who is six foot
one and 212 years old.

Herb Score

117

I've got ten pairs
of training shoes
– one for every
day of the week.

Samantha Fox

In a sense it's a one-man show...
except there are two men involved,
and a third man, the goalkeeper.

John Motson

—◆—

It is now 22 minutes past 8.30.

Lynn Russell

—◆—

We talked five times. I called him
twice and he called me twice.

Larry Brown

That's inches away from
being millimetre perfect.

Ted Lowe

———

I started with nothing and
I still have most of it.

Michael Davis

———

It's clearly a budget.
It's got a lot of numbers in it.

George W. Bush

At least 50 per cent of the
population are men, and
the rest are women.

Harriet Harman

———•———

Chile has three options.
They could win or they could lose.

Kevin Keegan

———•———

You guys have to run a little
more than full speed out there.

Bill Peterson

Here's Moses Kiptanui, the 19-year-old Kenyan, who turned 20 a few weeks ago.

David Coleman

THE FAME GAME

I don't think anybody
should write his
autobiography until
after he's dead.

Samuel Goldwyn

I can do anything as long as
I don't have to speak.

Linda Evangelista

—◆—

Acting is easier and smoother
than singing – it's less drama.

Beyoncé Knowles

—◆—

Of course Jim Morrison is
dead now, which is a high price
to pay for immortality.

Gloria Estefan

125

As I said to the Queen recently,
I can't stand name-droppers.

Alan Whicker

This is the 46th interview I've
done about wanting privacy.

Glenda Gilson

POOR EXPLANATIONS

We're not retreating.
We're advancing in
another direction.

General Douglas MacArthur

If you take out the killings,
Washington actually has
a very low crime rate.

Marion Barry

It isn't pollution that's harming our
environment. It's the impurities in
our air and water that are doing it.

Dan Quayle

The streets are safe in
Philadelphia. It's only the people
who make them unsafe.

Frank Rizzo

First, it was not a strip bar, it was an erotic club. And second, what can I say? I'm a night owl.

Marion Barry

We don't necessarily discriminate. We simply exclude certain types of people.

Colonel Gerald Wellman

I haven't committed a crime. What I did was fail to comply with the law.

David Dinkins

There is no housing
shortage in Lincoln
today – just a rumour
that is put about by
people who have
nowhere to live.

G. L. Murfin

I was under medication when I made
the decision to burn the tapes.

Richard Nixon

———◆———

The only thing that remains unsolved
is the resolution of the problem.

Thomas Wells

TV HOWLERS

So Carol, you're
a housewife and a
mother. And have
you got any children?

Michael Barrymore

Did you write the words or the lyrics?

Bruce Forsyth

If you or any member of your
family has been killed...

TV law commercial, Florida

Anything that's violent in TV
is a crime against humanity and
they should shoot the man
in the head responsible.

Ted Turner

OFF TARGET

Boxing is all about
getting the job done
as quickly as possible,
whether it takes 10
or 15 or 20 rounds.

Frank Bruno

That's the fastest time ever run
– but not as fast as the world record.

David Coleman

Ian Rush is perfectly fit, apart
from his physical fitness.

Mike England

You've got to get your first
tackle in early, even if it's late.

Ray Gravell

The only time they seem to get
the ball is when they give it away.

Ian St John

———

It may have been just going
wide, but nevertheless it was
a great shot on target.

Terry Venables

———

Yes, he misses a few – but he gets
in the right places to miss them.

Bill Shankly

MOVIE MADNESS

What the film business
really needs is
some new clichés.

Samuel Goldwyn

You can hardly tell where the computer models finish and the real dinosaurs begin.

Laura Dern on *Jurassic Park*

It's not the time it takes to take the take that takes the time. It's the time it takes between the takes that takes the time.

Steven Spielberg

Don't pay attention to critics. Don't even ignore them.

Samuel Goldwyn

If you don't have a psychiatrist
in Hollywood people
think you're crazy.

Patrick Bergen

◆

I just want to be normally insane.

Marlon Brando

◆

I think that the film *Clueless* was
very deep. I think it was deep in the
way that it was very light. I think
lightness has to come from a very
deep place if it's true lightness.

Alicia Silverstone

MEMORY LIKE A SIEVE

Sure Ronald Reagan
promised to take
senility tests – but
what if he forgets?

Lorna Kerr-Walker

I'll never forget what's his name.

Leslie Wolfson

I never forgive, but I always forget.

Arthur James Balfour

I have a grand memory for forgetting.

Robert Louis Stevenson

I think therefore I am... I think.

Howard Schneider

❧

I remember so clearly us going into
hospital so Victoria could have
Brooklyn. I was eating a Lion bar.

David Beckham

A MATTER OF LIFE
AND DEATH

Sadly, the immortal
Jackie Milburn
died recently.

Cliff Morgan

Please provide the date
of your death.

IRS letter

For most people, death comes
at the end of their lives.

Greater London Radio broadcaster

If your parents never had children,
chances are you won't either.

Dick Cavett

Capital punishment is our
society's recognition of the
sanctity of human life.

Orrin Hatch

—◆—

Suicide is a real threat to
health in modern society.

Virginia Bottomley

—◆—

We are sorry to announce that Mr
Albert Brown has been quite unwell,
owing to his recent death, and is
taking a short holiday to recover.

Parish magazine

Your food stamps will
be stopped because
we received notice
that you passed away.
May God bless you.
You may reapply if
there is a change in
your circumstances.

Department of Social Services, South Carolina

Sure there have been
injuries and deaths
in boxing – but none
of them serious.

Alan Minter

HOLD THE
FRONT PAGE

Supreme Court
rules that murderers
shall not be
electrocuted twice
for the same crime.

Cleveland Daily News

Lack of brains hinders research.

Columbus Dispatch

Weather forecast: precipitation in the morning, rain in the afternoon.

Detroit Daily News

On Sunday 5 April 1998, following a courageous fight for life, Catherine Thomas, surrounded by family, died at home – and she's bloody annoyed.

Obituary notice in Cardiff newspaper

Police chased
the getaway cat
for 40 miles.

Daily Mail

Concealed weapons charge
filed against nude dancer.

Headline in *La Mesa*, a California newspaper

Police in Hawick yesterday called
off a search for a 20-year-old man
who is believed to have frowned after
falling into the swollen river Teviot.

The Scotsman

Stopping otter hunting is
unlikely to benefit otters.

Field magazine

According to Colonial War Memorial staff, the woman was brought in after the accident for obliteration.

Fiji Daily Post

For sale: 1960 hearse. Original body.

Newspaper notice

The Labour Department said the increase in unemployment last month resulted from workers losing their jobs.

Keystone Heights newspaper

Most hotels are already
booked solid by people,
plus 5,000 journalists.

Bangkok Post

❦

Man shot neighbour with machete.

Miami Herald

TELL IT LIKE IT IS

You cannot
fashion a wit out
of two half-wits.

Neil Kinnock

Fiction writing is great, you can
make up almost anything.

Ivana Trump

———————

I will go to the opening of
anything, including a toilet seat.

Andy Warhol

———————

You could put all the talent I had
into your left eyelid and still not
suffer from impaired vision.

Veronica Lake

I believe in the discipline of silence so much I could talk for hours about it.

George Bernard Shaw

I write as a sow piddles.

Wolfgang Amadeus Mozart

I worked my way up from nothing to a state of extreme poverty.

Groucho Marx

There's no way Ryan Giggs
is another George Best.
He's another Ryan Giggs.

Denis Law

The president has kept all the
promises he intended to keep.

George Stephanopolous

Quite frankly, teachers are the only
profession that teach our children.

Dan Quayle

It's not so much a thankless task,
it's more a job with no thanks.

Colin Baker

———

The world is more like it is now
than it has ever been before.

Dwight Eisenhower

———

Those are the sort of doors that
get opened if you don't close them.

Terry Venables

I have nothing to say and I'm
saying it. That's poetry.

John Cage

Most of my clichés aren't original.

Chuck Knox

When people say less is more I
say more is more. Less is less.

Dolly Parton

It's a very good
historical book
about history.

Dan Quayle

NO BRAINER

If we were supposed
to live for ever, then
we would live for ever,
but we cannot live for
ever, which is why I
would not live for ever.

Miss Alabama 1994

I owe a lot to my parents,
especially my mother and father.

Greg Norman

I've learnt a lot of life skills
here – like boiling an egg.

Glyn Wise

The reason there is so little
crime in Germany is because
it's against the law.

Alex Levin

We all get heavier
as we get older
because there's a
lot more information
in our heads.

Vlade Divac

When I was young and irresponsible
I was young and irresponsible.

George W. Bush

———

The present tax on shoe leather is
putting an intolerable burden on the
bare-footed peasantry of Ireland.

Sir Boyle Roche

———

I think we agree that the past is over.

George W. Bush

Of all the things I've lost, it's
my mind I miss the most.

Ozzy Osbourne

— ✦ —

The Baggio brothers, of
course, aren't related.

George Hamilton

— ✦ —

I've seen *Much Ado About
Nothing* three times. It's a
great play. I'm not used to that
kind of culture and stuff.

Pamela Anderson

BAD ADVICE

Never use a long word
when a diminutive
one will do.

William Safire

An electric vote isn't worth
the paper it's written on.

Paul Delaney

—◦—

Smoking kills. And if you're
killed you've lost a very
important part of your life.

Brooke Shields

—◦—

If you haven't set off yet,
the best thing to do is turn
back and go home.

Anne Nightingale

Insomnia is a bad problem, but not one worth losing a night's sleep over.

Goronwy Jones

There's nothing the
matter with being
sick that getting
well can't fix.

Peg Bracken

ANATOMY LESSON

They've got old
shoulders on
their heads.

J. P. R. Williams

A brain scan revealed Andrew
Caddick is not suffering from
a stress fracture of the shin.

Jo Sheldon

Sometimes you open your
mouth and it punches you
straight between the eyes.

Ian Rush

Achilles tendons are a
pain in the butt.

David O'Leary

Some people are born with
natural false teeth.

Robert Robinson

Sonny Liston has a very unusual
injury: a dislocated soldier.

Henry Cooper

The doctors X-rayed my
head and found nothing.

Dizzy Dean

This is Vicente
Fernandez of
Argentina. You'll
notice that he walks
with a slight limp.
This is because he
was born with one
leg shorter than
the other two.

Roddy Carr

Monica Seles has so much
control of the racquet with
those double-handed wrists.

Virginia Wade

Michael Owen – he's got
the legs of a salmon.

Craig Brown

Danny, as you know, was
hospitalised last week
after complaining about
chest and sideburns.

Ned Martin

STUFF AND NONSENSE

A proof is a proof.
What kind of proof?
It's a proof. A
proof is a proof.
And when you have
a good proof, it's
because it is proven.

Jean Chrétien

If you walk backwards, you'll find out
that you can go forwards and people
won't know if you're coming or going.

Casey Stengal

———•———

I'll tell you one fact. It may be
boring, but it's rather interesting.

Barbara Cartland

———•———

Something that I was not aware
had happened suddenly turned
out not to have happened.

John Major

We're going to move left and
right at the same time.

Jerry Brown

———•———

If the Welsh only knew more
philosophy, what brilliant
philosophers they'd make.

Dai Evans

———•———

There's something about having a
horse between my knees that makes
it easier to sort out a problem.

Ronald Reagan

There are 127 varieties of nuts,
and Mia Farrow is 116 of them.

Roman Polanski

—◆—

I don't think there's anyone bigger
or smaller than Maradona.

Kevin Keegan

MIXED-UP METAPHORS

I can see the carrot
at the end of
the tunnel.

Stuart Pearce

The pendulum has gone full circle.

Jimmy Young

❦

Many clubs have a question
mark in the shape of an axe-
head hanging over them.

Malcolm McDonald

❦

When I say that Alex Ferguson
needs to stand up and be
counted, I mean that he needs
to sit down and take a good
look at himself in the mirror.

Gary Mabbutt

I would have thought that,
whichever way you slice the cake,
the government has certainly got
itself into an almighty pickle.

Jimmy Young

For some time now, the government
have been tightening the screws
on the terrorists from both
ends of the political rainbow.

Alex McLeod

Before a storm in a teacup
brews, nip it in the bud.

Russell Grant

Mr Speaker, I smell a rat. I see him
forming in the air and darkening
the sky, but I'll nip him in the bud.

Sir Boyle Roche

If you let that sort of thing go on,
your bread and butter will be cut
right out from under your feet.

Ernest Bevin

He's not the sharpest
sandwich in the picnic.

Tony Cascarino

＊

That's the way the cookie bounces.

Vic Schiro

＊

If you can't stand the heat of the
dressing room, get out of the kitchen.

Terry Venables

The toes you stand on today may
be attached to the legs that support
the arse you have to kiss tomorrow.

Watt Nicoll

The world is my lobster.

Keith O'Neill

STATING THE OBVIOUS

It is white.

George W. Bush describing the White House

We're now living in the
age in which we live.

Ann Burdie

Her decision was quite decisive.

John Cole

Food is an important part
of a balanced diet.

Fran Lebowitz

To me, the greatest book of all
time is the Bible because there's
some religious stuff in it.

Jim Rosenberg

The people in the navy look
on motherhood as being
compatible with being a woman.

James R. Hogg

Hang a thief while he's young and
he'll no steal when he's auld.

Lord Robert MacQueen Braxfield

You're the spitting image of yourself.

A fan to Billy Connolly

———◆———

When a man is asked to make
a speech, the first thing he has
to decide is what to say.

Gerry Ford

———◆———

It needs to be stated that the
poor are poor because they
don't have enough money.

Keith Joseph

CONTRARY MARYS

He died in his sleep
so he doesn't know
he's dead yet. If he
wakes up, the shock
will probably kill him.

Biddie McGrath

I will not tolerate intolerance.

Bob Dole

I want everybody to tell me the truth,
even if it costs them their jobs.

Samuel Goldwyn

I am not French. *Au contraire.*

Samuel Beckett

I'm an atheist, thank God.

Luis Buñuel

I don't believe in astrology. I'm a
Sagittarian and we're sceptical.

Arthur C. Clarke

I'm not superstitious – touch wood.

Dannie Abse

Being a millionaire is a bit
like being poor, except that
you have a lot of money.

Griff Rhys-Jones

Let this be a silent protest that will
be heard throughout the country.

Tim Leddin

I've got to follow them;
I am their leader

Alexander Ledru-Rollin

I don't blame anyone, except
perhaps all of us.

Willie Whitelaw

❧

When I came home I expected a
surprise and there was no surprise
for me so of course I was surprised.

Ludwig Wittgenstein

❧

We have to believe in free
will. We have no choice.

Isaac Bashevis Singer

God give me patience,
but make it fast.

Rosaleen Linehan

When I pick a team I
don't pick the 11 best,
I pick the best 11.

Brian Kerr

ASK A STUPID QUESTION...

Isn't it weird that I'm getting all emotionable?

Jessica Simpson

I don't even understand the
off-side rule, so how can I be
expected to understand a
Manchester United contract?

Victoria Beckham

I'm not indecisive.
Am I indecisive?

Jim Scheibel

What is a Liberal Democrat?

Helen Adams

I believe you're a fourth generation chef. What did your father do?

Lucy Freud

How could I have an IQ of 25 when I'm only 23?

Helen Adams

I am no playboy.
What is a playboy anyway?

Prince Andrew

What's Wal-Mart?
Do they sell like,
wall stuff?

Paris Hilton

www.summersdale.com